Charlotte Perkins Gilman

A Collection of Poems by Charlotte Perkins Gilman
(In This Our World, Suffrage Songs and Verses)

e-artnow 2019

Charlotte Perkins Gilman

A Collection of Poems by Charlotte Perkins Gilman

(In This Our World, Suffrage Songs and Verses)

e-artnow, 2019
Contact: info@e-artnow.org
ISBN 978-80-273-3182-6

Contents

Then This

The news-stands bloom with magazines,
They flame, they blaze indeed;
So bright the cover-colors glow,
So clear the startling stories show,
So vivid their pictorial scenes,
That he who runs may read.

Then This: It strives in prose and verse,
Thought, fancy, fact and fun,
To tell the things we ought to know,
To point the way we ought to go,
So audibly to bless and curse,
That he who reads may run.

Arrears

Our gratitude goes up in smoke,
In incense smoke of prayer;
We thank the Underlying Love,
The Overarching Care —
We do not thank the living men
Who make our lives so fair.

For long insolvent centuries
We have been clothed and fed,
By the spared captive, spared for once,
By inches slain instead;
He gave his service and is gone;
Unthanked, unpaid, and dead.

His labor built the world we love;
Our highest flights to-day
Rest on the service of the past,
Which we can never pay;
A long repudiated debt
Blackens our upward way.

Our fingers owed his fathers dead —
Disgrace beyond repair!
No late remorse, no new-found shame
Can save our honor there:
But we can now begin to pay
The starved and stunted heir!

We thank the Power above for all —
Gladly we do, and should.
But might we not save out a part
Of our large gratitude,
And give it to the power on earth —
Where it will do some good?

How Doth The Hat

How doth the hat loom large upon her head!
Furred like a busby; plumed as hearses are;
Armed with eye-spearing quills; bewebbed and hung
With lacy, silky, downy draperies;
With spread, wide-waggling feathers fronded high
In bosky thickets of Cimmerian gloom.

How doth the hat with colors dare the eye!
Arrest-attract-allure-affront-appall!
Vivid and varied as are paroquets;
Dove-dull; one mass of white; all solid red;
Black with the blackness of a mourning world —
Compounded type of "Chaos and Old Night"!

How doth the hat expand: wax wide, and swell!
Such is its size that none can predicate
Or hair, or head, or shoulders of the frame
Below thIs bulk, this beauty-burying bulk;
Trespassing rude on all who walk beside,
Brutally blinding all who sit behind.

How doth the hat's mere mass more monstrous grow
Into a riot of repugnant shapes!
Shapes ignominious, extreme, bizarre,
Bulbous, distorted, unsymmetrical —
Of no relation to the human head —
To beauty, comfort, dignity or grace.

Shape of a dishpan! Of a pail! A tub!
Of an inverted wastebasket wherein
The head finds lodgment most appropriate!
Shape of a wide-spread wilted griddlecake!
Shape of the body of an octopus
Set sideways on a fireman's misplaced brim!

How doth the hat show callous cruelty
In decoration costing countless deaths;
Carrying corpses for its ornaments;
Wreath of dead humming-birds, dismembered gulls,

The mother heron's breastknot, stiffened wings;
Torn fragments of a world of wasted life.

How doth the hat effect the minds of men?
Patient bill-payers, chivalrously dumb!
What does it indicate of woman's growth;
Her sense of beauty, her intelligence,
Her thought for others measured with herself,
Her place and grade in human life to-day?

Thanksgiving

I never thought much of the folks who pray
The Lord to make them thankful for a meal
Expecting Him to furnish all the food
And then provide them with the gratitude
They haven't grace to feel.

I never thought much of this yearly thanks,
Either for what once happened long ago,
Or for "our constant mercies." To my mind
If we're to thank a Power that's daily kind,
Our annual's too slow.

Suppose we spread Thanksgiving-hand it round —
Give God an honest heartful every day;
And, while we're being thankful, why not give
Some gratitude to those by whom we live —
As well as stingy pay?

Thanksong

Thankful are we for life
And the joy of living.
Baby-pleasure of taking;
Mother-glory of giving.

Thankful are we for light
And the joy of seeing.
Stir of emotion strong,

And the peace of being.

Thankful are we for power,
And the pride ensuing;
Baby-pleasure of having,
Father-glory of doing.

Love

Not the child-god of our most childish past,
Nor sympathy, nor worship, passionless;
Nor gratitude, nor tenderest caress:
Nor the post-mortal glamor priests have cast
With "This to hope! Surrender what thou hast!"
These are but parts and can but partly bless;
We in our new-born common consciousness
Are learning Law and Life and Love at last.

The age-old secret of the sphinx's holding,
Incarnate triumph, infinitely strong;
The mother's majesty, grown wide and long,
In the full power and fire of life's unfolding;
The conscious splendor and ripe joy thereof—
Glad world-wide, life-long service-this is Love!

Steps

I was a slave, because I could not see
That work for one another is our law;
I hated law. I work? I would be free!
Therefore the heavy law laid hands on me
And I was forced to work in slavery —
Until I saw.

I was a hireling, for I could not see
That work was natural as the breath I drew,
Natural? I would not work without the fee!
So nature laid her heavy hands on me
And I was forced by fear of poverty —
Until I knew.

Now I am free. Life is new-seen, recast
To work is to enjoy, to love, to live!
The shame and pain of slavery are past,
Dishonor and extortion follow fast,
I am not owned, nor hired, full-born at last,
My power I give.

Child Labor

The children in the Poor House
May die of many an ill,
But the Poor House does not profit
By their labor in the mill!

The children in the Orphanage
Wear raiment far from fine,
But no Orphanage is financed
By child labor in a mine.

The Cruel Law may send them
To Reform School's iron sway,
But it does not set small children
To hard labor by the day.

Only the Loving Family,
Which we so much admire,
Is willing to support itself
On little children's hire.

Only the Human Father,
A man, with power to think,
Will take from little children
The price of food and drink.

Only the Human Mother —
Degraded, helpless thing!
Will make her little children work
And live on what they bring!

No fledgling feeds the father-bird!
No chicken feeds the hen!
No kitten mouses for the cat —
This glory is for men.

We are the Wisest, Strongest Race —
Loud my our praise be sung! —
The only animal alive
That lives upon its young!

We make the poverty that takes
The lives of babies so.
We can awake! rebuild! remake! —
And let our children grow!

His Crutches

Why should the Stronger Sex require,
To hold him to his tasks,
Two medicines of varied fire?
The Weaker Vessel asks.

Hobbling between the rosy cup
And dry narcotic brown, —
One daily drug to stir him up
And one to soothe him down.

Get Your Work Done

Get your work DONE, to remember, —
Nothing can take it away,
Then shall the sun of December
Shine brighter than goldenest May.

What is the Spring-time of flowers for?
Why does the sunshine come down?
What are the harvest-day hours for
But fruit? In the fruit is the crown.

Why should we grieve over losses?
Why should we fret over sin?
Death is the smallest of crosses
To the worker whose harvest is in.

A Central Sun, a song

Given a central sun-and a rolling world;
Into the light we whirl-and call it day;
Into the dark we turn-and call it night;
Glow of the dawn-glory of midday light —
Shadow of eve-rest of the fragrant night
And the dawn again!

Given a constant Power-and a passing frame;
Into the light we grow-and call it life;
Into the dark we go-and call It death;
Glory of youth-beauty and pride and power —
Shadow of age-rest of the final hour —
And are born again!

Locked Inside

She beats upon her bolted door,
With faint weak hands;
Drearily walks the narrow floor;
Sullenly sits, blank walls before;
Despairing stands.

Life calls her, Duty, Pleasure, Gain —
Her dreams respond;
But the blank daylights wax and wane,
Dull peace, sharp agony, slow pain —
No hope beyond.

Till she comes a thought! She lifts her head,
The world grows wide!
A voice-as if clear words were said —
"Your door, o long imprisoned,
Is locked inside!"

Here Is The Earth

Here is the earth: As big, as fresh, as clean,
As when it first grew green;
Our little spots of dirt walled in,
As easy to outgrow as sin,
In the swift, sweet, triumphal hour
Of nature's power.

We have not hurt the world: Still safe we rest
On that great loving breast.
Proud, patient mother! Strong and still!
Our little years of doing ill
Lost in her smooth, unmeasured time
Of life sublime.

We need not grieve, nor kneel our faults to own;
She has not even known
That we offended! Our misdeeds
She covers with one summer's weeds:
Her love we thought so long away —
Is ours to-day.

And here are we. Our bodies are as new
As ever Adam grew:
Replenished still with daily touch,
By the fair mother, loving much.
Glad living things! Still conscious part
Of earth's rich heart!

And for the soul which these fair bodies give
Increasing room to live —?
It is the same soul that was born
In the dim, lovely, unknown morn
Of Nature's waking-the same soul —
Still here, and whole!

Strong? 'Tis the force that governs ring on ring
Where quiet planets swing.
Glad? 'Tis the joy of riotous flowers
And meadow-larks in May, now ours,

Ours endlessly-to have-to give —
To all who live!

No grief behind have we, no fear before
But only more and more
The splendid passion of the soul
In new creation to unroll:
All life, poured new in all the lands,
Through our glad hands!

The "Anti" And The Fly

The fly upon the Cartwheel
Thought he made all the Sound;
He thought he made the Cart go on —
And made the wheels go round.

The Fly upon the Cartwheel
Has won undying fame
For Conceit that was colossal,
And Ignorance the same.

But to-day he has a Rival
As we roll down History's Track —
For the "Anti" on the Cartwheel
Thinks she makes the Wheels go back!

Two Prayers

Only for these I pray,
Pray with assurance strong:
Light to discover the way,
Power to follow it long.

Let me have light to see,
Light to be sure and know,
When the road is clear to me
Willingly I go.

Let me have Power to do,
Power of the brain and nerve,
Though the task is heavy and new
Willingly I will serve.

My prayers are lesser than three,
Nothing I pray but two;
Let me have light to see,
Let me have power to do.

Before Warm February Winds

Before warm February winds
Arouse an April dream —
Or sudden rifts of azure sky
Suggest the bluebird's gleam;

Before the reddening woods awake,
Before the brooks are free —
Here where all things are sold and hired,
The driven months we see.

Wither along our snow-soiled streets,
Or under glass endure,
Fruits of the days that have not come,
Exotic-premature.

I hear in raw, unwelcome dawns
The sordid sparrows sing,
And in the florist's windows watch
The forced and purchased spring.

Little Leafy Brothers

Little, leafy brothers! You can feel
Warmth o' the sun,
Cool sap-streams run,
The slow, soft, nuzzling creep
Of roots sent deep,
And a close-anchored flowing
In winds smooth-blowing.
And in the Spring! the Spring!
When the stars sing —
The world's love in you grows
Into the rose!

Little hairy brothers! You can feel
The kind sun too;
Winds play with you,
Water is live delight;
In your swift flight
Of wings or leaping feet
Life rushes sweet —
And in the Spring! the Spring!
When the stars sing —
The world's love stirs you first
To wild, sweet thirst,
Mad combat glorious, and so
To what you know
Of love in living. Yes, to you first came
The joy past name
Of interchange-the small mouth pressed
To the warm, willing breast.

But O! the human brothers! We can feel
All, all below
These small ones know;
Earth fair and good,
The bubbling flood
Of life a-growing-in us multiplied
As man spreads wide;
Not into leaves alone,
Nor flesh and bone,
But roof and wall and wheel
Of stone and steel;
Soft foliage and gorgeous bloom
Of humming loom;
And fruit of joy o'er-burdened heart
Poured forth in Art!

We can not only leap in the sun,
Wrestle and run,
But know the music-measured beat
Of dancing feet,
The interplay of hands-we hold
Delight of doing, myriad-fold.
Joy of the rose, we know —
To bloom-to grow! —
Joy of the beast we prove —
To strive-to move!
And in the Spring! the Spring!
When the stars sing,
Wide gladness of all living men
Comes back again,
A conscious universe at rest
In one's own breast!
The world's love! Wholly ours;
Through breathing flowers,
Through all the living tumult of the wood,
In us made good;
Through centuries that rise and fall —
We hold it all!
The world's love! Given music, fit
To carry it.
The world's love! Given words at last, to speak,
Though yet so weak.
The world's love! Given hands that hold so much,
Lips that may touch!
The worlds's love! Sweet! —it lies
In your dear eyes!

A Walk Walk Walk

I.

I once went out for a walk, walk, walk,
For a walk beside the sea;
And all I carried for to eat, eat, eat,
Was a jar of ginger snaps so sweet,
And a jug of ginger tea.

For I am fond of cinnamon pie,
And peppermint pudding, too;
And I dearly love to bake, bake, bake,
A mighty mass of mustard cake,
And nutmeg beer to brew.

II.

And all I carried for drink, drink, drink,
That long and weary way,
Was a dozen little glasses
Of boiled molasses
On a Cochin China tray.

For I am fond of the sugar of the grape,
And the sugar of the maple tree;
But I always eat
The sugar of the beet
When I'm in company.

III.

And all I carried for to read, read, read,
For a half an hour or so,
Was Milman's Rome, and Grote on Greece,
And the works of Dumas, pere et fils,
And the poems of Longfellow.

For I am fond of the Hunting of the Snark,
And the Romaunt of the Rose;
And I never go to bed
Without Webster at my head
And Worcester at my toes.

Ode To A Fool

"Let a bear robbed of her whelps meet a man, rather than a fool in his folly." —
Prov. 17th, 12th.

Singular insect! Here I watch thee spin
Upon my pin;
And know that thou hast not the least idea
I have thee here.
Strange is thy nature! For thou mayst be slain
Once and again;
Dismembered, tortured, torn with tortures hot —
Yet know it not!
As well pour hate and scorn upon the dead
As on thy head.
While I discuss thee here I plainly see
Thee sneer at me.

Marvellous creature! What mysterious power
In idle hour
Arranged the mighty elements whence came
Thy iron frame!
In every item of thy outward plan
So like a man!
But men are mortal, dying every day,
And thou dost stay.
The nations rise and die with passing rule,
But thou, O Fool!
Livedst when drunken Noah asleeping lay,
Livest to-day.

Invulnerable Fool! Thy mind
Is deaf and blind;
Impervious to sense of taste and smell
And touch as well.
Thought from without may vainly seek to press
Thy consciousness;
Man's hard-won knowledge which the ages pile
But makes thee smile;
Thy vast sagacity and blatant din
Come from within;
Thy voice doth fill the world from year to year,

    Helpless we hear.

Wisdom and wit 'gainst thee have no avail;
O Fool-All Hail!

The Sands

It runs-it runs-the hourglass turning;
Dark sands glooming, bright sands burning;
I turn-and turn-with heavy or hopeful hands;
So must I turn as long as the Voice commands;
But I lose all count of the hours for watching the sliding sands.

Or fast-or slow-it ceases turning;
Ceases the flow, or bright or burning —
"What have you done with the hours?" the Voice demands.
What can I say of eager or careless hands? —
I had forgotten the hours in watching the sliding sands.

Water-lure

We who were born of water, in the warm slow ancient years,
Love it to-day for all we pay
Of terror and loss and tears.

The child laughs loud at the fountain, laughs low in the April rain,
And the sea's bright brim is a lure to him
Where a lost life lives again.

Aunt Eliza

(This was done by two persons, in alternate lines, as a game.)

Seven days had Aunt Eliza
Read the Boston Advertiser,
Seven days on end;
But in spite of her persistence
Still she met with some resistance
From her bosom friend.

Thomas Brown, the Undertaker,
Who declared he'd have to shake her,
Daily called at ten;
Asking if dear Aunt's condition
Would allow of his admission,
With his corps of men.

Aunt Eliza heard him pleading,
Ceased an instant from her reading,
Softly downward stole;
Soon broke up the conversation,
Punctuating Brown's oration,
With a shower of coal.

The Cripple

There are such things as feet, human feet;
But these she does not use;
Firm and supple, white and sweet,
Softly graceful, lightly fleet,
For comfort, beauty, service meet —
There are feet, human feet,
These she does with scorn refuse —
Preferring shoes.

There are such things as shoes-human shoes;
Though scant and rare the proof;
Serviceable, soft and strong,
Pleasant, comely, wearing long,
Easy as a well-known song —
There are shoes, human shoes,
But from these she holds aloof —
Prefers the hoof!

There are such things as hoofs, sub-human hoofs,
High-heeled, sharp anomalies;
Small and pinching, hard and black,
Shiny as a beetle's back,
Cloven, clattering on the track,
There are hoofs, sub-human hoofs,
She cares not for truth, nor ease —
Preferring these!

When Thou Gainest Happiness

When thou gainest happiness,
Life's full cup of sweetest wine;
Dost thou stop in grieving blind
Over those dark years behind?
Bitter now, rebellious, mad,
For the things thou hast not had —
Before everything was thine?

Dost not rather wonder why
Nearing blaze of joy like this,
Some prevision had not lit
Those dark hours with hope of it?
That thou couldst in patient strength
Have endured that sorrow's length —
Nothing —to the coming bliss!

Now, awaken! Look ahead!
See the earth one garden fair!
See the evils of to-day
Like a child's faults put away!
See our little history seem
Like a short forgotten dream!
See a full-grown rising race
Find our joy their commonplace!
Find such new joy of their own
As our best hopes have not known!
And take shame for thy despair!

For Fear

For fear of prowling beasts at night
They blocked the cave;
Women and children hid from sight,
Men scarce more brave.

For fear of warrior's sword and spear
They barred the gate;
Women and children lived in fear,
Men lived in hate.

For fear of criminals to-day
We lock the door;
Women and children still to stay
Hid evermore.

Come out! You need no longer hide!
What fear ye now?
No wolf nor lion waits outside —
Only a cow.

Come out! The world approaches peace,
War nears its end;
No warrior watches your release —
Only a friend.

Come out! The night of crime his fled —
Day is begun;
Here is no criminal to dread —
Only your son!

The world, half yours, demands your care,
Waken, and come!
Make it a woman's world, safe, fair,
Garden and home!

His Agony

A Human Being goes past my house
Day after day, hour after hour,
Screaming in agony.
It is dreadful to hear him.
He beats the air with his hands, blindly, despairingly.
He shrieks with pain.
The passers-by do not notice him.
The woman who is with him does not notice him.
The policeman does not notice him.
No ambulance comes ringing.
No doctor rushes out of a house-no crowd collects.
He screams and screams.
No one notices him.
I bear him coming again.
It is terrible-one day after another.
I look out of my window.
Yes-the same Human Being-the same agony.
I cannot bear it. I rush down-out into the street.
I say to the woman who is with him —
"Why do you not do something?"
She says there is nothing to be done. She resents my interference.
She is a hired person, hired by the owner of the Human Being.
That is why no one does anything —
We dare not interfere with the Owner.
He is a very young Human Being,
That is why no one notices —
We are used to the sound of agony and the indifference of hired persons.

Brain Service

We offer our hearts to God, contrite and broken;
Why not offer our brains, whole and alive?
Why follow the grovelling words wailing old races have spoken?
Bow and submit, when we ought to resist and strive!

What is this "heart" that you offer? A circulator,
An organ that quivers and starts at the fears of the hour.
Why not offer your head? And hold it straighter?
Bring to the service of God your noblest power?

When we learn to credit Him with our great ideals, and greater —
When we all stand up at last, stop kissing the rod —
When we bring the brains of to-day to seek and serve the Creator —
God will look better to us, and we shall look better to God.

The Kingdom

"Where is Heaven?" asked the Person.
"I want Heaven-to enjoy it;
I want Heaven, recompensing
For the evils I have suffered —
All the terrible injustice,
All the foolish waste and hunger —
Where is Heaven? Can I get there?"

Then the Priest expounded Heaven:
"Heaven is a place for dead men;
After you are dead you'll find it,
If" —and here the Priest was earnest —
"*If* you do the things I tell you —
Do exactly what is ordered!
It will cost you quite a little —
You must pay a price for Heaven —
You must pay before you enter."

"Am I sure of what I'm getting?"
Asked the mean, suspicious Person.
"What you urge is disagreeable;
What you ask is quite expensive;
Am I sure of getting Heaven?"

Then the Priest prepared a potion,
Made of Concentrated Ages,
Made of Many Mingled Feelings —
Highest Hope and Deepest Terror —
Mixed our best and worst together,
Reverence and Love and Service,
Coward Fear and rank Self-Interest —
Gave him this when he was little,
Pumped it in before the Person
Could examine his prescription.
So the Person, thus instructed,
Now believed the things he told him;
Paid the price as he was able,
Died-the Priest said, went to Heaven —
None came back to contradict him!

*

"We want Heaven," said the People;
We believe in God and Heaven;
Where God is, there must be Heaven;
God is Here-and this is Heaven."

Then they saw the earth was lovely;
Life was sweet, and love eternal;
Then they learned the joy of living,
Caught a glimpse of what Life might be,
What it could be-should be-would be —
When the People chose to have it!

Then they bought no further tickets
Of the sidewalk speculators;
They no longer gave their children
The "spring medicine" of Grandma.
They said, "We will take no chances
Of what happens after dying;
We perceive that Human Beings,
Wise, and sweet, and brave, and tender,
Strong, and beautiful, and noble,
Living peaceably together,
In a universal garden,
With the Sciences for Soldiers,
With the Allied Arts for Angels,
With the Crafts and Trades for Servants,
With all Nature for the Teacher,
And all People for the Students,
Make a very pleasant Heaven.
We can see and understand it,
We believe we'd really like some;
Now we'll set to work and make it!

So they set to work, together,
In the Faith that rests on Knowledge,
In the Hope that's born of Wisdom.
In the Love that grows with Practise
And proceeded to make Heaven.

*

And God smiled. He had been tired
Of the everlasting dead men,
Of the hungry, grasping dead men;
He had always wanted live ones —
Wanted them to build the Kingdom!

Heaven Forbid!

When I was seventeen, you'd find
No youth so brash as I;
Things must be settled to my mind,
Or I'd know why!

I knew it all, and somewhat more,
What I believed was true;
The future held no task in store
I could not do!

If I had died in my youthful pride —
And no man can say when —
Should I have been immortal
As I was then? (Heaven forbid!)

When I was forty-two I stood
Successful, proud and strong;
Little I cared for bad or good —
My purse was long.

My breakfast, newspaper and train, —
My office, —the Exchange —
My work, my pleasure, and my gain —
A narrow range.

If I had died in my business pride —
And no man can say when —
Should I have been immortal
As I was then? (Heaven forbid!)

Now I am old, and yet I keep
Intelligent content;
I wake and sleep in the quiet deep
Of disillusionment.

I don't believe, nor disbelieve —
I simply do not know.
I fear no grave-no heaven crave —
Am quite prepared to go.

But when I die-and I would not stay,
Though a friend should show me how,
Shall I become immortal,
As I am now? (Heaven forbid!)

The Puritan

"Where is God?" I cried. "Let me hear!"
"I long for the voice of God!"
And I smote and trod
On all things clamoring near;
Small voices dear,
That wept and murmured and sung
Till my heart was wrung;
That shrieked, shrieked loud and clear,
As I with hammer and sword
Slew them in the name of the Lord.
Where is God?" I cried. "Let me hear!"
But my ears were ringing yet
With cries I could not forget;
The blood was flowing still,
From the thing I could not kill;
A smothered sobbing cry
Filled all the red, wet earth, the cold, hard sky —
God came not near.

Then long I lived alone,
On the desolate land; a stone
On the thing I could not kill.
I bent to my hardened will
All things that lived below;
I strove to climb above,
To the land of living love
I had dreamed of long ago,
But I could not see-not know.
"O God!" I cried, "Come near!
Speak! Let thy servant hear!
Have I not utterly slain
With tears of blood, with sweat of pain,
In this base heart of mine
All voices old and dear-to hear but Thine!
And if there struggleth still
The thing I could not kill,
Have I not put a stone
On its head? O Thou alone
Whom I would follow and fear —
Speak! Let Thy servant hear!"

Silent I lay, and weak;
Then did the darkness speak;
"Child of the World! My love
Is beneath as well as above!

Thou art not always led
By a light that shines ahead!
But pushed by an impulse blind —
A mighty Power behind!
Lifted, as all things grow,
By forces from below!
Fear not for thy long mistake —
Listen! And there shall wake
The voice that has found the way
From the beginning, upward ever, into the light of day!
Lo! I am with thee still —
The thing thou couldst not kill!

The Malingerer

Exempt! She "does not have to work!"
So might one talk
Defending long, bedridden ease,
Weak yielding ankles, flaccid knees,
With, "I don't have to walk!"

Not have to work. Why not? Who gave
Free pass to you?
You're housed and fed and taught and dressed
By age-long labor of the rest —
Work other people do!

What do you give in honest pay
For clothes and food?
Then as a shield, defence, excuse,
She offers her exclusive use —
Her function-Motherhood!

Is motherhood a trade you make
A living by?
And does the wealth you so may use,
Squander, accumulate, abuse,
Show motherhood as high?

Or does the motherhood of those
Whose toil endures,
The farmers' and mechanics' wives,
Hard working servants all their lives —
Deserve less price than yours?

We're not exempt! Man's world runs on,
Motherless, wild;
Our servitude and long duress,
Our shameless, harem idleness,
Both fail to serve the child.

May Leaves

My whole heart grieves
To feel the thrashing winds of March
On the young May leaves —
The cold dry dust winds of March
On the tender, fresh May leaves.

The Room At The Top

There is room at the top?
Ah yes! Were you ever there?
Do you know what they bear
Whose struggle does not stop
Till they reach the room at the top?

Think you first of the way,
How long from the bottom round, —
From the safe, warm, common ground
In the light of the common day —
'Tis a long way. A dark way.

And think of the fight.
It is not so hard to stand
And strive off the broad free land;
But to climb in the wind and night,
And fight, —and climb, —and fight!

And the top when you enter in!
Ah! the fog! The frost! The dark!
And the hateful voices-hark!
O the comfort that you win!
Yes, there's room at the top. Come in!

A Bawling World

A SESTINA.

Be not impatient with the bawling world! —
The clatter of wild newsmongers, the cry
Of those in pulpits, the incessant speech
From many platforms, and the various prayers
Of tale-tellers all striving for our ears,
And poets that wait and gibber-they have cause.

For all this noise there is a natural cause,
Most natural of all that move the world,
The one that first assails a mother's ears
When loud a lusty infant learns to cry,
An inarticulate insistent prayer
But serving that first need as well as speech.

Reason and love combine to give us speech,
But this loud outcry has a simpler cause,
The same that prompts the roaming jackal's prayer
And fills the forests of the untamed world
With one long, jarring hungry piteous cry —
Such cry as still attacks our weary ears.

We long for human music in our ears,
For the clear joy of well-considered speech,
And the true poet's soul-uplifting cry
To lead us forward, striving for the cause
Of liberty and light for all the world —
And hear but this confused insensate prayer.

Vainly we seek to fly this ceaseless prayer —
To find some silent spot-to stop our ears: —
There is no place in all the groaning world
Where we can live apart from human speech:
and we, while speech is governed by this cause,
Are infants "with no language but a cry."

It is for food that all live creatures cry,
For food the sparrow's or the lion's prayer,
And need of food is the continuing cause,
Of all this deafening tumult in our ears.

Had we our food secure —! Then human speech
Might make mild music, and a wiser world!

*

Poor hungry world! No wonder that you cry;
Elaborate speech reduced to primal prayer:
To save our ears let us remove the cause!

O Faithful Clay!

O faithful clay of ancient brain!
Deep graven with tradition dim,
Hard baked with time and glazed with pain,
On your blind page man reads again
What else were lost to him.

Blessed the day when art was found
To carve and paint, to print and write,
So may we store past memory's bound,
Make our heaped knowledge common ground.
So may the brain go light.

Oh wondrous power of brain released,
Kindled-alive-set free;
Knowledge possessed; desire increased;
We enter life's continual feast
To see-to see-to see!

We Eat At Home

RONDEAU

We eat at home; we do not care
Of what insanitary fare;
So long as Mother makes the pie,
Content we live, content we die,
And proudly our dyspepsia bear.

Straight from our furred forefather's lair
The instinct comes of feeding there;
And still unmoved by progress high
We eat at home.

In wasteful ignorance we buy
Alone; alone our food we fry;
What though a tenfold cost we bear,
The doctor's bill, the dentist's chair?
Still without ever asking why
We eat at home.

The Earth's Entail

No matter how we cultivate the land,
Taming the forest and the prairie free;
No matter how we irrigate the sand,
Making the desert blossom at command,
We must always leave the borders of the sea;
The immeasureable reaches
Of the windy wave-wet beaches,
The million-mile-long margin of the sea.

No matter how the engineers may toil,
Nature's barriers and bulwarks to defy;
No matter how we excavate and spoil,
De-forest and denude and waste the soil,
We must always leave the mountains looming high;
No human effort changes,
The horizon-rolling ranges
Where the high hills heave and shoulder to the sky.

When a child may wander safely, east or west,
When the peaceful nations gossip and agree.
When our homes are set in gardens all at rest,
And happy lives are long in work loved best,
We can leave our labor and go free;
Free to go and stand alone in,
Free for each to find his own in.
In the everlasting mountains and the sea.

Alas!

Have those in monstrous hats no glimmering dream
Of the high beauty of the human head,
House of the brain: seat of the sentient soul;
Haloed for sainthood; crowned for royalty;
Bright-ringed with roses, wreathed with noble bays,
Most beautifully bound with shining hair.

Alas for the soft glory they have lost!
Alas for the Ashantee wigs they wear!
Nor plait nor coil nor ringlet, but a mass
Of shorn dead hair from poorer women's heads.
Of bulging wire and hard, stiff, glittering bands.
A heap no loving hand would long to touch.

This body is the glory of the world;
The head the body's crown; but we on this
Plant like a fool's-cap these preposterous forms.
Alas for women's folly; and alas
For man, who likes his women to be fools,
And carefully has bred them to this end.

"The Outer Reef!"

(A Picture by Paul Dougherty.)

Who dares paint daylight?
The bright white light of flaming noon?
No blur of shadow, mist or haze,
Just the whole unobstructed blaze
Of hot mid-June.

No screen of leafage;
The keen clean green of summer sea;
Dazzle of surf in mid-day light,
The very sound of the surges' fight,
Broad-open-free.

The earth all stillness,
Noon hush on the pastures' height;
Turf topped cliffs with faces bare,
Bones of the earth unveiled to air,
Heat-breakers-light.

To-morrow Night

Marginal mile after mile of smooth-running granite embankment,
Washed by clean waters, clean seas and clean rivers embracing;
Pier upon pier lying wide for the ships of all seas to foregather,
Broad steps of marble, descending, for the people to enter the water,
White quays of marble, with music, and myriad pleasure-boats waiting;
Music of orchestras playing in blossoming parks by the river,
Playing on white-pillared piers where the lightfooted thousands are dancing,
Dancing at night in the breeze flowing fresh from the sea and the river;
Music of flute and guitar from the lovers afloat on the water,
Music of happy young voices far-flying across the bright ripples,
Bright with high-glittering ships and the low rosy lanterns of lovers,
Bright with the stars overhead and the stars of the city beside them,
Their city, the heaven they know, and love as they love one another.

The Waiting-Room

The Waiting-room. With row on row
Of silent strangers sitting idly there,
In a large place expressionless and bare,
Waiting for trains to take them other-where;
And worst for children, who don't even know
Where they're to go.

The Waiting-room. Dull pallid Patients here,
Stale magazines, cheap books, a dreary place;
Each Silent Stranger, with averted face,
Waiting for Some One Else to help his case;
and worst for children, wondering in fear
Who will appear.

Only Mine

They told me what she had done —
Of her life like a river free:
Teaching and showing with tender truth,
Giving her light to age and youth,
Till fathers and mothers and children grew
To listen and learn and see
What the village had come to be;
How they had no sickness, young or old,
And had lost but one from all their fold;
For all the people knew
How to keep life strong and true;
And I asked her how had her love begun
To ripen and reach to every one.

She lifted a royal head,
Standing straight, as a tree;
While troops of little ones clustered and clung
To raiment and hand and knee.
"Should I not be glad," said she,
"In health and beauty and joy like this?
Babies by hundreds to cuddle and kiss;
A happier town was never sung;
A heaven of children for old and young;
There is only one that is dead —
It was only mine," she said.

A Question

Why is it, God, that mother's hearts are made
So very deep and wide?
How does it help the world that we should hold
Such welling floods of pain till we are old
Because when we were young one grave was laid —
One baby died?

In How Little Time

In how little time, were we so minded,
We could be wise and free-not held and blinded!
We could be hale and strong-not weak and sickly!
Could do away with wrong-and do it quickly!

Riches of earth, enough for all our keeping;
Love in the heart, awake, no longer sleeping;
Power in the hand and brain for what needs making;
Joy in the gift of power, joy in the taking!

In how little time could grow around us
A people clean and fair as life first found us!
One with the under-earth, in peaceful growing,
One with the over-soul, in doing, knowing.

Labor a joy and pride, in ease and beauty;
Art that should fill at last its human duty;
This we could make and have, were we not blinded!
In how little time-were we so minded!

The Socialist And The Suffragist

Said the Socialist to the Suffragist:
"My cause is greater than yours!
You only work for a Special Class,
We for the gain of the General Mass,
Which every good ensures!"

Said the Suffragist to the Socialist:
"You Underrate my Cause!
While women remain a Subject Class,
You never can move the General Mass,
With your Economic Laws!"

Said the Socialist to the Suffragist:
"You misinterpret facts!
There is no room for doubt or schism
In Economic Determinism —
It governs all our acts!"

Said the Suffragist to the Socialist:
"You men will always find
That this old world will never move
More swiftly in its ancient groove
While women stay behind!"

"A lifted world lifts women up,"
The Socialist explained.
"You cannot lift the world at all
While half of it is kept so small,"
The Suffragist maintained.

*

The world awoke, and tartly spoke:
"Your work is all the same;
Work together or work apart,
Work, each of you, with all your heart —
Just get into the game!"

Worship

How does it feel? —
The drawing of the magnet on the steel?
All else gives way;
No rivets hold, no bars delay,
Called in that overwhelming hour,
From far and near they fly and cling,
Allied, united, clustering;
And the great pulsing currents flow
Through each small scattered scrap below.
Scattered no more;
One with that all compelling core;
One absolute, one all alive with power.

How does it feel? —
The swift obedient utmost flight
Of radiant sky-wide waves of light,
Far couriers of the central sun,
Crossing a million miles as one —
Still going-going —
Limitless joy that needs no knowing
Each last least flickering ray
One with the Heart of Day.

The Little White Animals

We who have grown Human-house-bodied, cloth-skinned,
Wire-nerved and steam-heated —alas! we forget
The poor little beasts we have bandaged and pinned
And hid in our carpet-lined prisons! —and yet
Though our great social body be brickwork and steel,
The little white animals in it, can feel!

Humanity needs them. We cannot disclaim
The laws of the bodies we lived in before
We grew to be Human. In spite of our frame
Of time-scorning metals, the life at its core,
Controlling its action and guarding its ease,
Is the little white animal out of the trees!

It is true that our soul is far higher than theirs;
We look farther, live longer, love wider-we *know;*
They only can feel for themselves-and their heirs;
We, the life of humanity. Yet, even so,
We must always remember that soul at its base
Looks out through the little white animal's face.

If they die we are dead. If they live we can grow,
They ply in our streets as blood corpuscles ply
In their own little veins. If you cut off the flow
Of these beasts in a city, that city will die.
Yet we heighten our buildings and harden our souls
Till the little white animals perish in shoals.

Their innocent instincts we turn to a curse,
Their bodies we torture, their powers we abuse,
The beast that humanity lives in fares worse
Than the beasts of the forest with nothing to lose.
Free creatures, sub-human —they never have known
The sins and diseases we force on our own.

And yet 'tis a beautiful creature! —tall-fair —
With features full pleasant and hand-wooing hair;
Kind, docile, intelligent, eager to learn;
And the longing we read in its eyes when they burn

Is to beg us to use it more freely to show
To each other the love that our new soul can know.

Our engines drive fast in earth, water and air;
Our resistless, smooth-running machines still unroll,
With brain-work unceasing and handiwork fair,
New material forms for each step on the soul;
But that soul, for the contact without which it dies,
Comes closest of all through that animal's eyes.

Many Windows

Many minds are many windows,
Varied are their views;
Each of us, if lonely, knows
Only what one window shows —
Can no further choose.

any minds are many windows,
One the light divine,
We may freely move and range,
Wide our windows may exchange, —
Come and look through mine!

In A Much

The Christian arose upon Christmas Day
And solemnly cleared his score:
He called on the sick, to the needy gave alms,
And entered the prison door.

He lent to his friends, gave away his old coat
Was never by sinners enticed,
And handed the man who complained of a throat
A cup of cold water-iced.

He bestowed on a newsboy a new pair of shoes,
And quoted in pious glee:
"In as much as ye've done it to one of these least
Ye have done it unto me."

*

That night he dreamed upon judgment Day:
Men's hearts were all in their throats;
To his pained surprise he was hustled away
And herded among the goats!

"Oh Lord," he cried, "there is some mistake,
I have always remembered Thee!"
But the world's neglected children rose
And gazed reproachfully.

And a voice replied, "Thy punishment take;
Thy duty thou didst not see!
In as much as ye have NOT done it to ONE
Ye have NOT done it unto me."

Love's Highest

Love came on earth, woke, laughed and began his dominion.
Strong? Just the Force of Creation. Glad? Merely Joy of Existence.
Love cast about for Expression-for work, which is Love in Expression,
And the fluctuant tissues of life began burgeoning, blooming and
fruiting.
Up through dim ages laughed Love, flowing through life like a fountain,
Pouring new forms and yet newer, filling each form with new passion,
Playing with lives like a juggler, life after life, never dropping;
Till a new form was developed: Humanity came: it was daylight.

Love laughed aloud, rose in splendor, offered up hymns of thanksgiving.
"Now I have room for expression! Here is a vehicle worthy!
Life that is lovelier far than all these poor blossoms and creatures;
Life that can grow on forever, unlimited, changeful, immortal.
Here I can riot and run through a thousand warm hearts in a moment,
I can flash into glories of art! I can flow into marvels of music!
I can stand in Cathedrals and Towers, and sit splendid, serene, in fair
cities!
These exquisite, limitless beings shall radiate love from their faces,
Shall uphold it with emulous arms, and scatter it wide with their
fingers,
Shall build me, through ages and ages, new forms and new fields of
expression!
I have worked through the mosses and grasses till the world was all
sweetened with roses,
Warm-clothed with the soft-spreading forests, and fed with ripe wheat
and red apples;
I have worked with fur-children and feathered, till they knew the
delights of my kingdom;
I have shown, thousand-fold, throughout Nature, my
Masterpiece-Glory-the Mother!
Now love shall pour like the sunlight, shall cover the earth like the
ocean,
Love encompassing all, as the air does, not only in fragrance and color,
Not only in Nature and Mothers, but now, in this Crown of Creation —
Latest fruit of the Tree Everlasting, this myriad-featured fulfillment —
With unlimited force I shall fill them, in unnumbered new voices be
uttered,
By millions and millions and millions they shall pour out their love in
their labor,
And the millions shall love one another.

CPSIA information can be obtained
at www.ICGtesting.com
Printed in the USA
LVHW080334090819
627083LV00005B/32/P